The Leadership Voyage

Navigating the Tenets of Greatness

S. Michael Hoelscher

Following Seas Media, LLC

Copyright © 2025 Following Seas Media, LLC.

All rights reserved.

No part of this publication may be reproduced, distributed, or transmitted in any form or by any means, including photocopying, recording, or other electronic or mechanical methods, without the prior written permission of the publisher. Exceptions are made for brief quotations used in reviews, articles, or scholarly works, provided full credit is given to the book and Following Seas Media, LLC.

For permissions or inquiries, contact: permissions@FollowingSeasMedia.com

ISBN-13: 979-8-9930600-2-6

Published by Following Seas Media LLC. Printed on demand.
Following Seas Media, LLC
Info@FollowingSeasMedia.com

Disclaimer: This book is a work of the author's imagination and research. While names, characters, places, events, and incidents may be fictionalized or used fictitiously, any resemblance to actual persons, living or dead, or actual events is coincidental. Where nonfiction material is included, it is provided for general informational and educational purposes only and should not be relied upon as legal, financial, medical, or other professional advice. Readers are encouraged to seek guidance from qualified professionals for advice specific to their circumstances. The author and publisher disclaim any liability arising directly or indirectly from the use or application of the contents of this book.

Disclosure: The narrative text in this book was authored by a human. AI-assisted tools were used as supplementary aids in drafting, editing, and idea development, but do not replace authorship. Final creative control and responsibility for the content remain with the author and Following Seas Media, LLC. Cover art and design elements may include AI-assisted and human-modified components.

> Self-control is a strength.
> Right Thought is mastery;
> Calmness is power.
> Say unto your heart, "Peace be still!"

— JAMES ALLEN, *AS A MAN THINKETH*

This book is both inspired by and built upon the timeless truths found in Allen's work.

May these tenets continue the ripple he began.

To the Bridge, the Deck, and the Watch Below

No one commands the helm alone.

To those upon the Bridge who first cast the vision and forged the quiet discipline in me, I offer my deepest thanks. To my mother, Marilyn, and my father, Gus: yours were the first steady hands I watched. You taught me to walk in the world with purpose, to hold fast to truth, to labor with care. You did not chart my course, but you taught me how to read the stars. And that, in the end, was everything.

To those on the Deck, my shipmates of my life — Jason, Steve, Greg (may he rest in peace), and Mickey: no storm ever felt as fierce with you nearby. Through silence and laughter alike, you proved yourselves more than shipmates. You are the kind I would trust at the wheel in the blackest hour. No need for ceremony; you simply showed up. And kept showing up. That is its own kind of heroism.

To the Watch Below, my children, Connor, Haley, Branson, and Paul, if I have weathered storms, it was so you would have a clearer sky. All I have learned, I place at your feet, not as answers but as instruments. I offer these pages not as a legacy, but as a lantern, light enough, I hope, to guide your own voyage when the winds rise.

And to Amanda, my calm harbor, my restless sail. Where I doubted, you stood. Where I faltered, you reached. Not once did you demand that I arrive whole, only that I return honest. Yours has been the quiet faith that gave this vessel motion and meaning. I owe more than I can write.

This voyage, if it ever was mine, never was mine alone.

To all who held the line, bore the weight, or whispered strength when I was near spent, know this: whatever good comes from these words, it belongs to you too.

Sammy
Son. Friend. Father. Husband.

Preface

The way of a leader is not unlike the helm in open water, hands steady on the wheel, eyes scanning the horizon, heart always listening for the shift in wind. The wheel does not move on its own, nor is it held in rigidity. It requires presence. Subtlety. A constant conversation with forces both seen and unseen. Each decision is a tack, a minor adjustment, a deliberate choice that sends the whole vessel on a slightly different heading. Each moment brings the chance to redraw the chart, not in ink, but in action. What was once unknown, mysterious, and even frightening becomes, through the quiet persistence of will and the slow accumulation of wisdom, a map worth following.

In such a sea, the world throws distractions aplenty, and trends shimmer like mirages. Praise comes and goes with the tide. Titles are hoisted and lowered like flags in the wind. But none of that shows you true north. Fleeting fashions offer no compass. Their shine fades in the salt and sun. What endures, what truly endures, are truths. Not theories, not slogans, not borrowed wisdom polished for applause. Truths. Eternal. Luminous. Not loud, but steady. Like the stars above, present whether we see them or not, faithful when all else drifts.

These twenty truths, this little book of stars, is no decoration. It is not a gallery of good intentions or a clever framework to display in a conference room. It is a set of bearings. Anchors when the storm has its say. Sails when the winds of change stir restlessness in the crew. A compass when the dark is thick, and every heading feels like guesswork. These truths will not calm the sea. But they will keep you from capsizing. They offer not ease, but orientation.

Authentic leadership begins not with applause or assignment. It is not granted by vote nor sealed by rank. It begins in solitude, in the quiet decision to act, to serve, to carry. Before the title. Before the team. Before the recognition. It begins in the interior. A mind made still. A heart turned outward. A soul is braced for weight. Real leaders do not rise because they chase the helm. They rise because they could no longer bear to stand by.

To lead is to listen. To serve. To make yourself a safe place for others. A handhold when the deck is slick. A calm voice when the storm roars. The strongest among us are not those who command the most, but those who lift the most. They bear burdens. They hold the line. They show up.

And sometimes, the bravest thing a leader can do… is nothing at all. To resist the urge to push forward. To heave to, to stop, to hold position, to wait out the gale while others clamor for progress. To protect the ship, the crew, and the mission, even if it means delaying your own arrival. Stillness is not weakness. It is wisdom with its hand on the brake.

This book does not offer a checklist. It is not a manual. It is not to be recited for approval or mounted in a boardroom. These tenets must be lived. Not once, but daily. Not loudly, but deeply. You must carry them when no one is watching. You must return to them when you have drifted. They will become yours only through trial. Through error. Through the sacred repetition of doing the right thing when it costs you.

You are not a passenger on this voyage. You never were. You are the navigator. You are the wind-reader, the sail-trimmer, the mapmaker. James Allen said it plainly, and he was right: "They are makers of themselves." So too are you the maker of your leadership, forged not in the knowing, but in the doing.

Let these truths be your stars. Let them shine, not to be admired, but to be followed.

The Call to Lead

Leadership does not wait for a crown. It begins the moment someone sees that something must be done and does not look away.

It is not granted by rank, nor summoned by applause. It stirs in silence, in that small inward voice that asks, "If not me, then who?" And it is answered not with noise, but with movement. Quiet. Steady. Sure.

To lead is not to declare oneself worthy, but to accept responsibility where others defer it. Not in pride, but in purpose. Not for gain, but for good.

It arrives without ceremony. No one may notice when it begins. Perhaps not even you. But somewhere between hesitation and resolve, you stepped forward. And that was enough.

Leadership is not formed in title, but in character. It grows in the shadows of small decisions and is proven in storms no one sees coming. It reveals itself when others lean toward you, not out of duty, but trust.

Some obey commands to keep their wage. But they follow leaders because they see something deeper, integrity without pretense. A standard lived, not spoken. A willingness to carry weight, not cast it.

True leadership asks more than skill. It asks for the preparation of the soul. One must ready themselves to lead long before the moment demands it. This means learning. It means self-examination. It means living the values you claim, especially when no eyes are on you.

It is in the unseen habits, in how you listen, how you serve, how you speak to yourself, that leadership is first forged.

This is not a book about power. It is a book about weight.

Leadership carries cost. It may ask for your comfort. At times, it may ask for your certainty. It may even ask that you lose something to protect someone else. But to the one called to lead, no other path feels as right.

The twenty truths within these pages are not tactics. They are timbers. Shaped by storm. Weathered by use. Chosen by those who do not wish to lead for applause, but for something steadier, a purpose.

This is not a manual. It is a compass.

Let it guide you as you begin your voyage, a path not of perfection, but of presence. Where your choices ripple far beyond your own name. Where your strength becomes shelter. Where your voice becomes wind in another's sail.

Raise anchor. Fix your eyes on the horizon.

The time to lead is now.

I LEAD WITH INTEGRITY, CHOOSING THE HONEST COURSE EVEN WHEN THE EASIER PATH LIES IN REACH.

Lead with Integrity

Leadership, when anchored in integrity, does not drift. It holds fast, through calm, through squall, unmoved by applause, untouched by pressure. The true leader keeps to the course not because it is easy, but because it is right. Even when unseen. Even when inconvenient. They steer by a compass not made by others, but forged within.

It is no ornament. It is the very keel beneath the hull. Unseen, but bearing all.

Integrity is not declared. It is lived. It is not proved in speeches, but in small decisions. A leader who walks in step with their values does not need to convince anyone. Their life does the speaking. And where there is integrity, trust grows. Quietly. Deeply. And trust, once planted, holds more firmly than fear ever could.

The way of integrity is not an easy passage. It requires self-examination, often, not once. The leader watches not only their actions, but the heart behind them. They question their motives. They test their reasons. They ask: Am I choosing what is right, or what is simple?

This is not softness. It is strength under control. Because it takes courage, real courage, to do what is right when the cost is high or when the crowd turns away.

Integrity does not raise its voice. It does not seek credit. It asks only for truth, first from within, and then outward. To stand accountable, especially when it would be easier to explain, to excuse, or to hide, is to lead in its purest form. The one who takes full ownership, in failure as well as success, earns something no rank can give: the quiet loyalty of those around them.

Such integrity does more than shape a person. It shapes the world they touch. A leader who holds to principle becomes a shelter, a place where others can speak freely, offer honestly, and bring their full selves to the work. In that presence, people rise. Not by pressure, but by example. What is good becomes not rare, but regular. What is right becomes what is expected.

And in this, the culture shifts.

The crew steadies. Trust becomes the current that carries all things forward. Without it, even the most skilled hands will falter. With it, even storms are bearable.

Leadership cannot be separated from principle, not truly. Titles may be handed down, but character is revealed in trial. A leader's truest measure is not found in ease, but in adversity.

To lead with integrity is to sail by the stars. Fixed. Faithful. Unshaken by wind or wave.

And when all else is lost, it is enough to guide you home.

I CREATE SPACE FOR TRUTH TO BE SPOKEN WITHOUT FEAR, WHERE VOICES ARE RECEIVED WITH PATIENCE AND HEARD WITHOUT JUDGMENT.

Create a Safe Space for Honesty

The great leader does not merely direct. They shelter. They offer something rarer than authority: a harbor. A place steady and still. Free from the squall of ridicule. Untouched by the crosswinds of retaliation. In their presence, the calm people feel does not come from silence, but from knowing they are safe. And in that calm, truth takes root.

It is not enough to say, "Speak freely." People will not risk honesty where judgment waits in the wings. But in the shelter of a trusted captain, words begin to surface. Slowly at first, like ships on the far horizon. Dissent. Doubt. Admission of fault. Glimmers of something bold and untested. In this harbor, truth becomes not a risk, but a rhythm. And it begins, always, with the one at the helm.

Honesty is the tide that lifts the entire crew. When it flows freely, everything rises: ideas, morale, courage, clarity. People no longer hold back for fear of being misunderstood or punished. They begin to bring not just their hands, but their minds. And more importantly, their hearts. Challenges are faced earlier. Problems are named while they are still small enough to fix. Creativity awakens. Not in competition, but in communion.

The honest leader does not merely tolerate feedback. They invite it. They sit with it. They listen without flinching, especially when the words are sharp or unexpected. They are not pretending to sit still, they are actually doing it. They are not asking just to look polite, or to prove they listened. They ask because they are trying to make sense of what they missed, and they know they probably did. They have learned, sometimes the hard way, that a quiet truth can hit harder than any compliment. And letting it sit in the dark only makes it heavier.

To build a place where truth belongs, one must be brave. Consistently so. It is one thing to ask for candor. It is another to honor it, even when it stings. Even when it slows things down. Especially when it turns around and lands on your own shoulders. The ones who really mean it when they say, "Speak freely," do not flinch when someone disagrees. They do not take it as betrayal. They take it as proof the culture is working. Being corrected is not the same as being challenged. It does not mean someone is turning against you, it just means they care enough to speak up. And a hard truth, gently given, is still a gift.

But truth does not thrive on bravery alone. It needs repetition. It needs to be modeled. Often. In small ways and big ones. The way a leader reacts when someone admits a mistake matters. The way they acknowledge uncertainty matters. If truth is punished or minimized, people will retreat. And once that retreat begins, it is hard to reverse. Culture hardens quickly. Fear spreads quietly. And soon, silence takes root where trust once lived.

When truth is welcome, feedback moves both ways. Not as a weapon, not as a secret whisper, but as a steady current people can count on. It flows with clarity, not cruelty. It is offered with care and received with humility. In this climate, people are not guarded, they are growing. Disagreement sharpens rather than divides. Trust deepens. And the crew, no longer operating in isolation, moves as one.

Over time, this culture changes everything. Not just how people speak, but how they think. How decisions are made. How problems are approached. How setbacks are weathered. In a crew accustomed to honesty, ego softens. Blame fades. People begin to look forward instead of inward. And when the winds shift, they adjust. Together.

When honesty sticks around long enough to become normal, something deeper settles in. People start to trust, not just you, but the space. And in that trust, they loosen a little. Let themselves be real. And brave. The courage to risk. The clarity to focus not on self-preservation, but on shared success. The job stops being just tasks. It starts being about the people you do it with. The reasons you stay. The little things that make it feel like it matters.

Over time, honesty turns into something sturdier. People stop waiting to be told. They start holding themselves to the line, quietly, without a show. Not the kind that is forced. The kind that is chosen. They do not work harder out of fear. They step up because someone trusted them, and they do not want to break that trust. They start to name their own missteps. They speak up when things feel off. And they do so not to impress, but to protect the space that allows them to be human.

To lead with honesty is not about hanging posters that say "transparency matters." It is how you show up when someone tells you something hard. It is what you do when a mistake comes to light. It is letting people know, through how you listen, how you react, that truth has a place here. That their worth is not tied to getting it all right, but to being real enough to speak up.

Let honesty be what moves you forward. It will take your leadership farther than command ever will. And let your crew know, not through words alone, but through lived example, that the truth will always find harbor here.

I EMPOWER OTHERS THROUGH TRUST, GIVING RESPONSIBILITY NOT AS A BURDEN BUT AS A PATH TO EXCELLENCE AND STRENGTH.

Empower Others

A wise leader does not grip the helm alone. They do not hoard control as proof of competence, or mistake busyness for strength. They understand something simple and easily forgotten: the ship does not sail because one person pulls every line. It sails because hands are trusted, roles are honored, and each crew member is given something real to hold.

To empower is not to assign chores. It is to entrust a piece of the voyage. To look someone in the eye, even if only for a moment, and say, "This is yours now." No fanfare, no big speech. Just a quiet handoff that changes everything. And in that moment, something begins. Confidence takes root. The crew member is no longer just carrying out orders. They are carrying meaning.

A great leader sees more than what someone does. They notice what that person might grow into, if given the chance. They assign not only by skill, but by potential. Not merely to finish the task, but to stir something dormant, a deeper sense of agency, pride, and capability. That kind of assignment is not random. Real empowerment is never passive. It is thoughtful. Specific. Intentional. Shaped for the person, and for the moment they are in.

To delegate well requires discipline, the kind that looks slow from the outside. The kind that listens carefully, that waits for understanding before making the ask. It means noticing more than who speaks loudest. It means asking, quietly: What is ready to grow here? Who is quietly waiting to be trusted? It means watching how someone handles pressure, not just whether they perform. And then, placing them where they will stretch, but not snap.

But handing over responsibility is only the beginning. To truly empower, the leader must also learn to step back. They do not disappear, and they do not hover either. They simply step aside. Enough to let someone else steer. Enough to let them get it wrong and still find their way. There must be space, space to wrestle, to adjust, to figure it out. Freedom inside a frame. Structure without suffocation.

And yes, mistakes will come. The sea does not smooth itself for any crew. But a seasoned captain does not grab the wheel at the first wrong turn. They do not bark orders just to feel in control. They wait. They watch. They offer course corrections when it matters, but they let others learn. Even the wrong wind has lessons, if the sails are up.

Growth does not come through micromanagement. It comes through invitation. Through space. Through the trust that says, "You will figure this out. And I will be here, if you need me."

Empowerment is not only about being there when something goes wrong. It is just as much about being present when someone rises. When they step into a bigger version of themselves. When they surprise even their own expectations. The leader who sees this and says, "Well done," is not offering praise, they are laying ballast. They are grounding confidence. They are saying, without needing to explain it: You are seen. You belong here. Keep going.

And over time, something shifts. The crew stops waiting for permission. They begin to move. They do not move in chaos or rebellion. They move with care, with intent. They take ownership of their space. They look out for one another. They solve before being asked. Leaders start to emerge in every corner, not because they were chosen, but because they were trusted.

They are no longer just helping. They are leading, in their own way. To empower others is to carry vision in one hand and humility in the other. It is to know when to lead from the front, and when to step to the side. Letting go is not a weakness. It is wisdom. The strongest leaders are not measured by how much they hold. They are measured by how much they lift others up.

So let that be your measure, not how much you control, but how much you release. Not how loud your voice, but how many voices you make space for. Let your crew become more than assistants. Let them become stewards of the journey.

Trust boldly. Delegate with care. Empower without fear. And then watch the wind fill their sails.

I LIVE THE STANDARD I SET, LETTING MY ACTIONS SPEAK LOUDER THAN ANY COMMAND OR CLAIM.

Live the Standard

Real values do not need a spotlight. The strongest leaders I have seen do not talk about integrity all day, they just live it. It shows up in the pauses, in what they choose not to say, in the quiet consistency of their choices. Not as decoration, but as something woven into their tone, their timing, their smallest choices. They do not just stand on shore pointing out a direction. They step into it first, and by moving, they become the path.

It is not speeches that inspire. It is when words and actions finally match. You can feel it when what someone says and what they do begin to line up. The tension drops. People lean in a little more. It is not magic, it is just rare enough to matter. Trust begins. Not the kind of trust that only lasts when things are easy, but the kind that sticks when no one knows what comes next. When the storm hits, and you still believe in who is at the wheel. Charisma might attract, but alignment builds something that lasts.

At the center of lasting leadership is not force, but example. No one can call others to integrity while cutting corners when no one is watching. No one earns loyalty while pointing fingers and dodging blame. The crew is watching, not out of suspicion, but out of hope. They are not looking for flawlessness. They are looking for consistency. They want to see a line they can trace, from words to action, from ideals to behavior.

Words alone are sails without wind. They may look noble, but they will not move the ship. What fills the sails is repeated, grounded, visible action. The kind that holds even when no one is checking. People learn more from what a leader tolerates than from what they preach. They pay attention to what actually happens. You can say kindness matters, but if the loudest, harshest voice keeps getting promoted, people stop believing the talk. You can ask for excellence, but if half-effort gets a pass, that becomes the new normal. Culture does not shift with slogans, it shifts with what actually gets rewarded.

But when values are lived, not just when it is easy, but when it costs something, they become more than principles. They become part of the air. They shape the rhythm of the place. Respect, honesty, accountability… these stop being exceptions. They turn into the rhythm of daily life, not because anyone orders it, but because people see it happening.

To lead by example is to know that nothing is neutral. Every glance, every delay, every word, spoken or withheld, teaches something. Leadership never stops communicating.

Even in silence. Especially in silence. And when the pressure hits, when things go sideways, the crew does not flip to page seventeen of the handbook. They look at the leader. How are they moving? What are they choosing? Are they steady? Or are they slipping?

Adversity does not break true leadership. It shows what was really there all along. A calm presence in chaos settles more than panic. It spreads something quieter and stronger: belief. Not the kind built on wishful thinking, but the kind earned through steadiness. A look that says, "We have seen worse. We will get through this." And when that calm stays anchored in conviction, when the leader adapts without abandoning the standard, the crew learns something deeper. That it is possible to change course without losing who you are.

This kind of leadership does not just guide, it shapes. It becomes the undercurrent that pulls the culture forward, even when words are failing. Over time, the example becomes the rule. People begin to self-correct, not because they fear consequence, but because they have seen better. And they want to rise to it.

The smallest acts often land the deepest. You might never know how far a quiet decision reaches. How a moment of humility, or fairness, or quiet courage settles in someone's mind. But it does. People notice more than you think. Not because they want to catch mistakes, but because they are hoping to find someone worth trusting. Someone who means what they say. Someone real. A sign that leadership can still mean something. That it still stands for honor. For consistency. For carrying weight without needing praise.

To lead this way is to invite others into their own leadership. Not by critique. By example. The leader who expects much, but walks with grace, offers a space where people feel safe to grow, even when they fail. Their very presence says, "You have more in you. I see it."

They do not drag others forward. They draw them forward. That is a different kind of strength.

This is not about performance. It is not about being admired. It is about building something solid. A shared sense of character. A place where people do not just point to what they built, but how they built it. Where the way they got there matters just as much as the result. Maybe even more.

As the voyage continues, hold to this simple truth: we are always being watched. Not for flawlessness, but for consistency. Not for brilliance, but for steady truth in motion. Every small moment builds, or breaks, the trust we claim to carry. So live with clarity. Move with coherence. Let the line between who you are and how you lead fade away. Let your crew see the standard, long before they hear it. And in doing so, let your life become something others want to follow.

I CAST A VISION BOTH STEADY AND CLEAR, A GUIDING LIGHT THAT GIVES PURPOSE TO EACH TASK AND MEANING TO THE VOYAGE.

Inspire Vision and Purpose

A true leader does more than assign direction. They awaken it. They move beyond managing tasks and deadlines and begin shaping something larger, something lasting. A vision. A shared horizon the crew can fix their eyes on. A reason that justifies the effort, redeems the hardship, and gives the voyage its meaning. Not just what we do, but why we rise to do it, especially when the wind dies down or turns against us.

Vision is not the same as strategy. It is not numbers on a spreadsheet, or a glossy poster, or a slide at a meeting. It is quieter than that, and deeper. A vision is a call. A shared imagining of what could be. A light, even faint, that flickers on the horizon and reminds everyone that the course they sail has purpose.

Great leadership does not just steer the ship. It names the destination. And not just the one marked on maps, but the one that stirs the soul. The one that makes the hard days worth it. It says, "This is where we are going. This is what matters. And this is why your effort belongs here."

Without that clarity, crews drift. They work, but without conviction. They row, but without rhythm. The days blur. Frustrations get louder. Small setbacks begin to feel like something bigger. But when the vision is clear, and shared, every motion means something. Even pain starts to feel like progress. The storms do not go away, but at least they are pushing you toward a place that makes sense.

Vision steadies more than the plan. It steadies people. It quiets panic, restores will, gives breath when everything feels too tight. It reminds the crew: this struggle is not the whole story. It is just one part of the journey.

Visionary leadership is not about operating smoothly. It is about reaching. It dares to name a future worth working for, and then works backwards from there. But this kind of vision is not dictated from a corner office. The most durable visions are not handed down. They are discovered. They are shaped together.

Which is why wise leaders listen. Not just to take notes, but to understand. They listen to fears, to hopes, to the quiet things people do not always say out loud. They listen for what brings people pride, what keeps them loyal, what pulls them into motion. A vision that ignores the hearts of the people who carry it will never become more than a sentence. But a vision built through listening becomes something else entirely. A shared promise.

When the crew helps shape the course, it stops being the captain's idea. It becomes their own. And ownership is what turns intention into energy. They row harder, not because someone is watching, but because they believe in what they are rowing toward. And belief, once planted, becomes hard to shake.

Of course, even the clearest vision will face storms. Plans will fall apart. Timelines will shift. That is just part of the sea. But a real vision holds. It does not need perfect weather. Visionary leaders are not rigid. They do not pretend to have it all figured out. What they do is return, again and again, to what matters. They remind the crew what still stands. They adjust when needed, but they do not lose their direction.

This kind of leadership does more than reach a goal. It creates culture. It attracts people who want to build something that matters. And it pushes those people to grow. They stop seeing themselves as replaceable parts. They become carriers of purpose. The work starts to feel different. Sharper. More alive. The mission becomes real, not because it was predicted, but because people believed in it enough to make it so.

Vision does not just point forward. It lifts upward. It turns energy into movement. It aligns scattered effort. It helps people choose purpose over passivity. It does not just talk about the future, it makes people want to build it.

And so, as we continue our own leadership voyage, let us cast visions that move more than numbers. Let us dare to name goals that speak to the heart. Let us show the crew not only what must be done, but what could be, if all of us pull together.

What we offer has to go deeper than productivity. It has to carry purpose. Deeper than metrics. It has to carry meaning. Beyond plans. It has to spark belief. So cast your vision boldly.

I EMBRACE HUMILITY, ACKNOWLEDGING WHERE I FALL SHORT AND MEETING EACH TIDE WITH A MIND READY TO GROW.

Demonstrate Humility and Vulnerability

A leader's greatest strength is not how much they know. It is how willing they are to admit they do not know it all. To recognize one's humanity is not to shrink, it is to lead from something real. It means stepping away from the illusion of having every answer, and instead charting a course rooted in truth. The best leaders are not the ones pretending to be unbreakable. They know where they fall short, where things still wobble, and instead of hiding that, they lean into it. They try to get better, even if it is slow.

Humility does not mean shrinking away. It means you do not have to keep proving yourself every second. The leaders who carry it do not white-knuckle their control. They loosen their grip. They do not try to have all the answers, they leave space for others to step in. Saying "I am not sure" does not knock them down a peg. In a strange way, it pulls people closer. Because suddenly, things feel honest.

The kind of leadership that lasts usually starts with self-awareness. Not the checklist kind. The kind that catches you off guard in the middle of a normal day, makes you stop and think, "I missed that. I need to work on that." Not just to admire strengths, but to acknowledge blind spots. To ask, "Where am I falling short?" A leader has to be honest with themselves before they can ever hope to be honest with others. This inner work is invisible, but it anchors everything else. Without it, ego fills the gaps. Without it, trust breaks down.

But when a leader embraces humility, something shifts. The questions get better. The conversations get richer. The need to be right gives way to the need to understand. And the crew can feel it. They stop holding back. They speak up. Because the invitation feels real. Because the room feels safe.

There is courage in saying, "I got that wrong." Or, "I need help." Or simply, "What do you think?" These are not signs of failure. They are signs of someone still learning. Still open. Still human. And that humanity is not weakness. Vulnerability, in this light, is strength made visible. When a leader shares their struggles without performance, no dramatic confession, just honesty, it softens the air. The crew is no longer following a title. They are following a person. And in that person, they see pieces of themselves. So they show up more fully. They speak more freely.

In that kind of space, where people are allowed to be real, trust actually takes root. Not because everything is perfect, but because someone bothered to show up as they really are.

When a leader stops acting flawless, people relax. They think, "Maybe I do not have to be perfect either." And something softer, more honest, starts to grow in the room. They do not demand flawless performance. They ask for honesty. Effort. Growth. And they help create the conditions for that growth. They give feedback without fear. They offer encouragement without pretense. And they allow space for mistakes, as long as learning follows.

They become more than managers. They become mentors. Not just people who decide, but people who guide. These leaders do not protect their lessons like secrets. They pass them on. Especially the hard ones. They take what they have learned the hard way, and turn it into something useful for someone else. They give direction, not just correction. They slow down when needed. They make time. They open doors. And slowly, the whole crew lifts.

In this kind of culture, people do not just survive the work, they grow through it. Innovation shows up more often. Collaboration deepens. People share ideas more freely. Not because someone demanded it, but because someone made it safe to try. And the tone at the top made that safety possible.

That is the power of leading with humanity. It does not need to dominate. It does not need to impress. It makes room. It clears space. And it lasts.

When people feel seen, they stay. When they feel heard, they contribute. When they feel safe, they stretch. And the ship, once moved by a few strong hands, begins to surge forward on the strength of everyone aboard.

Leadership does not get stronger by hiding our humanity. It grows when we are brave enough to admit it.

So let us lead with open hands. Let us make space for our own imperfection, so others feel free to bring their whole selves too. Let us listen without rushing to respond. Let us learn without shame.

And let us remember this: those who follow are not looking for flawless leaders. They are looking for someone real. Someone honest. Someone they can grow with.

I SUPPORT AND ENCOURAGE MY CREW, CELEBRATING THEIR VICTORIES AND WALKING BESIDE THEM THROUGH THE HARD WEATHER.

Provide Support and Encouragement

A great leader does more than steer the ship, they lift the crew. Not with grand speeches. Not with hollow praise. But with presence. With recognition. With quiet, steady moments that remind someone: You matter. I see you.

Support is not about control. It is about placing strength beneath someone, not to keep them close, but to help them rise. And not because they owe you, but because they can.

When leadership is consistent and rooted in care, it becomes part of the structure. Something solid underfoot. Encouragement is not a nice-to-have. It is a stabilizer. It holds the rigging when the winds pick up. It says, even in the middle of the hard stuff, "You are not alone. I see the work. I believe in where this is headed."

Real recognition is fuel. Not the kind that burns quick and loud, but the kind that keeps a slow fire steady. The best leaders do not wait around for dramatic wins. They notice the little stuff. The small moments no one else sees. A quiet improvement. A repeated effort. The hundredth time someone showed up and tried again. They name it. Not with fanfare, but with something real. A look. A word. A quiet "I noticed." And somehow, that one small moment stays with a person longer than they expect. Maybe longer than the leader ever knows.

Because to be seen, truly seen, is no small thing. And to be lifted, slowly and steadily, does not just change the person. It changes the whole culture.

When people feel valued not only for what they deliver, but for who they are becoming, something clicks. Trust grows. Confidence settles in. The work stops being just work, it becomes shared. It starts to matter in a different way.

But support is more than kind words. It shows up in the tools you hand someone. In the time you make for their learning. In the way you stay calm when the plan goes sideways. It is not just praise, it is preparation. Listening without rushing. Standing nearby, not only when things go right, but when they begin to fray.

Support says, "You will not fall by yourself." Encouragement follows with, "I believe you can rise again." Together, they form something stronger than motivation. Not a fragile kind of positivity, but a flexible, grounded kind of belief.

Because people do not need a leader shouting directions from the shore. They need someone willing to wade into the mess, point toward the path, hand over what is needed, and remind them, gently, honestly, that they are more capable than they realize.

This is not about coddling. It is about investing. When people feel like their leader is invested in them, not just in the outcomes, they take more risks. They ask more questions. They stretch. Not out of fear, but out of courage. Because the ground beneath them feels solid.

And that steadiness multiplies. The culture begins to shift. Asking for help stops being seen as weakness. It becomes normal. Even smart. People start speaking up earlier. Communication stops being filtered and starts being real. They stop guarding themselves and start giving more of themselves, not to impress, but to contribute.

And when the storm comes, as it always does, all of that work pays off. The bounce-back is quicker. People trust the process. They trust each other. And that trust lasts longer than the moment.

Long after the project ends, someone remembers the time they were backed. The words that lifted them. The gesture that said, "You are not invisible." The time a leader stayed close, not to correct, but just to stand with them. Those moments become the hidden scaffolding. They hold the crew together when things get tight.

The leader who supports does more than maintain morale, they reinforce identity. They remind people of their worth. They create a space where people can give their full selves, skill, voice, and spirit. And when that happens, the crew does not just complete the voyage. They shape it.

Support turns possibility into progress. Encouragement turns hesitation into motion. And together, they build a crew that does not just survive the rough waters, but becomes stronger because of them.

This kind of leadership does not demand attention. But it earns respect. Because it lifts without strings. It celebrates without agenda. And it understands the long game: when we lift others, we all rise.

Let your leadership be felt not just in what you decide, but in how you care. Let your words build. Let your presence steady. Let your belief in others give them the wind they need.

In the end, it is not just the crew that rises. The whole vessel moves forward, stronger than it was.

I FOSTER UNITY, NOT THROUGH SAMENESS, BUT BY HONORING DIFFERENCE, SHAPING A WHOLE STRONGER THAN ITS PARTS.

Build a Culture of Collaboration

The strength of a crew does not come from sameness. It comes from unity, not the kind built on everyone thinking alike, but the kind shaped through shared effort and respect. A great leader does not expect every voice to echo their own. They expect the opposite. They welcome differences. They know disagreement is not a threat. It adds depth. In their presence, variety is not a problem to manage, but a strength to understand.

And it starts, always, with how they listen. Not the fake kind of listening, nodding while waiting to talk. Real listening. The kind that looks for what is true, even if it is not agreement. The best leaders are not thrown off by a perspective they do not share. They lean in. Not to win an argument, but to learn something they could not see before. That is the soil where collaboration takes root.

When people feel safe bringing what they have, not in fear, but in faith, something shifts. Work changes. It becomes something done with others, not just around them. Ideas stack instead of clash. They build like stones in a wall, different shapes, but stronger together. There is no need for uniformity. There is only the need for each voice to be welcomed and rightly placed.

True collaboration is not easy. It is effort that is shared. It is the hard, slow work of choosing to listen when it would be easier to decide. It means speaking with care and receiving disagreement without flinching. The leader does not force everyone into alignment. They set a tone. Calm. Curious. Open. And the crew adjusts, not out of pressure, but out of trust.

Some people speak fast, others need more time. A thoughtful leader gives space for both. There is no rush to reach the loudest opinion. Some of the best insights arrive late, unfolding only when the room quiets down. The leader's job is not to speed things up, it is to make space for things to surface.

So they wait. They resist the urge to fill every silence. They hold their voice just long enough to let others find theirs. They bring order not by taking control, but by anchoring the group with steadiness. And slowly, something forms. Not just a team, but a rhythm. Hands start reaching across roles. People step into conversations they once avoided. Ideas stretch across boundaries without needing permission.

Ownership spreads. The goal is no longer the leader's. It is everyone's. Because everyone had a hand in shaping it.

And the effects show up in small ways first. A hesitant idea offered without apology. A second voice adding, not competing. A teammate who once stayed quiet now leaning forward, ready to speak. These moments might seem ordinary. But they are signs of a culture shifting, not because of rules, but because of trust.

And in time, that trust ripples outward. Crews that learn to think together begin to build beyond themselves. Collaboration is no longer internal, it reaches into partnerships, shared projects, wider teams. The walls come down. Respect grows. What was once kept close is now given freely. And work done together, when done with care, always goes further.

Collaboration cannot be mandated. It has to be modeled. It is built in a thousand small decisions, who gets the mic, who gets the time, how disagreement is handled, how silence is treated. It becomes a habit. A rhythm. The undercurrent of everything the crew does.

And underneath it all is one quiet truth: someone listened first. Someone chose not to dominate the room. Someone held space. Someone set the tone by showing how trust is earned, not with certainty, but with humility.

Let your leadership be less about directing and more about making room. Not to control, but to connect. Not to rush, but to build strength. Not to prove your voice is the loudest, but to be sure no voice is lost.

Collaboration may not be the fastest path, but it is the strongest. And it is what holds when the wind picks up.

I LISTEN WITH CARE, HEARING NOT ONLY WORDS BUT THE HEART BEHIND THEM, AND LETTING EACH VOICE BE KNOWN.

Listen Actively

The leader who listens well does not just speak clearly. They bring their whole self to listening. Not to jump in with a reply, not to win a point, but simply to hear.

Words offered without real understanding are rarely helpful. But to pause, to listen without interrupting, without preloading a response, that is presence. That is strength. And that is where trust begins.

To listen fully, something inside has to go still. Not just the face, not just the hands, but the swirl of thoughts demanding attention. The point you want to make. The comeback forming. The judgment quietly slipping in. All of that has to be set aside, or you are not really listening, you are just waiting for your turn.

The wise leader finds that pause. They ease up on being right. They loosen their hold on certainty. They let the moment belong to the other person. And in that silence, something opens. You begin to hear not just the words, but everything wrapped inside them: the tension, the uncertainty, the flicker of hope hidden behind a shaky voice.

Real listening is slow. It takes time. It does not jump to conclusions. It holds space. It watches the speaker, not just their face, but their rhythm, their hesitation, what they choose not to say. And when done well, it becomes something rare: a refuge. A place where people stop guarding and start opening up.

When that happens, the tone shifts. People speak, not because they were called on, but because they know they will be received. That reception matters more than the answer. Because when someone feels truly heard, something deep begins to form: trust. Not the kind built on charm or clever words, but the kind rooted in stillness. In attention.

Listening is not passive. It is deeply active. It does not mean nodding politely. It means working to understand. Asking for clarity when something feels off. Repeating back what was said to check your grasp. Offering care instead of critique. Listening is not just about gathering data, it is about carrying something that matters. And what is carried that way must be handled with respect.

When leaders show up like this, it changes more than the conversation, it starts to change the culture. People begin to listen to each other. The tone becomes less defensive. More curious. Less wall-building, more bridge-building. Problem-solving becomes shared. Meetings get quieter in the best kind of way, less jockeying, more actual thinking. Not everyone will remember what the leader said, but they will remember how it felt to be heard. To not be brushed off. To have even a small concern treated with care.

That memory lingers. That is how belonging begins.

And so, the leader listens. Not just once, not only when it is easy, but as a way of leading. They listen when the room is full of energy, and when the silence drags. They listen when ideas are messy, and when emotions run high. They listen when the answers are not clear, and when things start to fall apart.

Because in those moments, especially, people are watching. They are listening to see if you are listening. And if you are, if you stay present, stay calm, stay with them, they will start to offer more. Not just words. But insight. Truth. Creativity. Commitment. All the things that only show up when people feel safe.

This is not some extra leadership skill. It is core. Listening changes decision-making. It slows it down, yes, but in a way that deepens it. Ideas are no longer limited to one perspective. The direction chosen is shaped by many. And what comes out of that is not just smarter, it is more connected. More owned.

To listen well is to say, without needing to say it: You matter. Your thought matters. You are not just here to follow, you are here to shape something with us.

The influence of this kind of leadership reaches beyond the moment. Long after the meeting ends, people will remember being heard. Even if nothing changed, even if the answer was "not yet," being listened to still shifts something.

So lead with your ears open. Let your words follow after. Let silence show care instead of doubt. And when the moment tempts you to jump in, pause. Because in the listening, you might find something you never would have thought to ask.

And in the quiet that follows… you will lead.

I STEER TOWARD THE GREATER GOOD, CHOOSING WHAT SERVES THE CREW, EVEN WHEN THE COURSE IS NOT THE EASIEST TO CHART.

Make Decisions for the Greater Good

Real leadership rarely looks heroic. It is not often loud. Most days it shows up as quiet choices made behind closed doors, with too little time, too many unknowns, and the weight of it all pressing down. And still, you choose, not for yourself, but for the ones counting on you. The strongest decisions are rarely the most visible. They do not come with applause. They take shape in silence, after hours of staring at imperfect options, after hearing the same points from five angles, after waking at 3 a.m. wondering what you have missed. That is where the greater good lives: in the pause between what is easy and what is right.

A wise leader resists the urge to grab the first clear path just to escape the pressure. They breathe, widen their view, and ask not just what will get them through today, but what decision, if made now, could make tomorrow better for everyone. It is not about self-preservation or polishing an image, but choosing what serves. And yes, it can be heavy, to feel all those eyes on you, some skeptical, some hopeful, some just needing to know they are still seen, that the compass being followed still has a human hand on it. Leadership at its best does not protect itself. It listens. It weighs. It bends toward what matters. That does not mean it always comforts. Some choices will upset people. Some will feel right but not good. That is part of the deal: choosing what holds, even when it hurts.

Pushback will come. That does not always mean people have lost faith; sometimes they simply cannot see what you can. You are not leading for agreement, but to keep the team whole under pressure, to keep the mission alive when the weather turns. So you make the call, not with bravado but with care, and when you do, you explain the why. Without spin. Without self-protection. You help people understand how you got there. And even when they would have chosen differently, trust begins to form around the way you decide, and that is what lasts.

Over time, choosing with the bigger picture in mind begins to echo in others. The crew starts asking different questions. They stretch their thinking beyond their own tasks. They take responsibility for more than their slice. Culture shifts, not because new slogans go up on the wall, but because people see it lived. You will not get every decision right; no one does. However, how you decide matters. The willingness to slow down when quick answers tempt, to ask for counsel, to check your motives, to ask, Who does this affect? What might they lose? That kind of steady thinking becomes leadership on its own.

And people notice. They start doing it too. The quiet "no," the tough "yes," the long explanation nobody asked for; these small moments add up. They form the spine of a team that trusts the process, of a system that does not buckle at the first hit, of a crew that knows how to hold together because they have seen it done. Maybe no one will remember that one hard call you made this week. Maybe it will not be anyone's highlight. But you will know. You will know you chose the call that kept someone safe, that steadied the hull so it would not crack later, that let the crew rest a little easier, even if they never knew why.

That is leadership. It will not make headlines. It makes things last. So, when the moment comes —and it will —take the long view. Look wider. Ask harder questions. Let the weight in. Then choose. Do it without chasing credit, simply because someone has to. And in that moment, that someone is you.

I REMAIN FLEXIBLE AND WATCHFUL, ADJUSTING OUR SAILS WITH FORESIGHT AND GRACE AS THE WINDS SHIFT.

Adaptability

The sea never holds still. Neither can the leader. To lead well is not to cling, it is to respond. The tide does not ask for permission. The wind will not wait until you feel ready. The wise leader does not fight the current just to prove they can. They read it, they feel it shift, and they adjust. Not out of fear, but because the ship that never changes course rarely makes it far. Adaptability is not weakness. It is wisdom moving in real time, a quiet step forward when the old road disappears and the new one has not fully revealed itself. To keep moving while holding your direction. To change without losing who you are.

Fighting every change is another way of clinging to yesterday. But chasing change for its own sake leaves you drifting. The grounded leader does neither. They notice what is shifting around them and hold to what must stay anchored within. When the horizon disappears and the next step feels uncertain, an adaptable leader does not panic. They take in what the moment offers, not just the obvious facts, but the undercurrents, the things not being said, what is beginning to wear thin. The decision they make is not a reaction, but a response, one that may come quickly, but is built from years of watching, learning, and listening.

Adaptability is not born in comfort. It is shaped in friction, when plans fall apart, when tools fail, when the way things used to work simply stops working. In those moments, the adaptable leader does not freeze or flail. They listen, they adjust, they try again. And still, they lead. There is no chart that tells you when to push ahead, when to hold still, or when to wait. That kind of knowing is not granted. It is earned. Tide by tide. Mistake by mistake.

Leaders who adapt well pay attention not just to numbers or shifting deadlines, but to the quiet changes in the people around them. They notice when someone goes silent, when motivation dips, when what once worked no longer connects. The signals are subtle, but they are there. These leaders do not cling to old ways simply because they are familiar. But they also do not throw everything out at the first challenge. They test. They question. They keep what is still solid and let go of what no longer serves. The crew notices. They see how the leader moves through uncertainty, how they stay calm even when things wobble. They follow not because they think the leader has all the answers, but because they see they are not pretending to. That honesty builds steadiness.

Adaptable leaders invite ideas without bracing for threat. They listen more when things get unclear. They soften their tone when tightness would only make things worse. They shift gears, not for effect, but because the moment calls for it. And that posture changes people. Others start loosening their grip too. Fear eases. The urge to control fades. People begin to move more freely. They speak with less caution. They try more. Risk more. The culture starts to breathe. It is not loud. It does not announce itself. But you can feel it in how the crew responds to setbacks, not with blame but with curiosity. They adjust. They reflect. They try again. Failure does not define them. It shapes them. And in the process, they grow stronger.

Adaptability, lived well, is not just a skill. It is a steady presence, a way of being that holds even when the wind shifts and the maps feel out of date. It reminds us that real strength does not always stand firm. Sometimes it moves, deliberately, gently, with eyes open and heart steady. That movement leads to more than short-term success: it leads to sustainability. A rigid leader eventually burns out, and a rigid crew eventually breaks. But those who adapt, slowly and wisely, without losing who they are, endure. They fall less. They learn faster. And when they do fall, they rise without shame.

So let the leader seek not to control every wave, but to prepare for its arrival. Not to rush through every change, but to meet it with presence. To remember that the course may shift often, but the voyage continues. Those who adapt with purpose will always find a way forward.

I TEND TO MY OWN SPIRIT, UNDERSTANDING MY EMOTIONS AND EXTENDING EMPATHY TO THOSE WHO JOURNEY WITH ME.

Emotional Intelligence

The wise leader does not govern by judgment alone, but by temperament too. Before leading others, they learn to lead themselves. Most leadership trouble does not start out there; it starts inside. A storm at sea can be managed. A storm in the heart, if ignored, can tear the vessel apart. To lead well is to feel deeply, and still stay steady. To walk beside others without being swept away by their tempests. To steady the tone when the room shakes. To hear fear without absorbing it. To carry pressure without passing it on.

This kind of leadership begins with self-awareness, not as a performance or a checkbox, but as a way of being. The emotionally intelligent leader notices when irritation rises, when judgment sharpens, when pride tries to take the wheel. They do not excuse it, but they do not bury it either. They listen inward first. That is where emotional intelligence begins, not in expression, but in understanding. From that inner understanding grows the rest: restraint in anger, gentleness in conflict, calm in disappointment, and warmth even when others grow cold. These are not soft traits. They are marks of someone who walked through fire and did not turn brittle.

Strength shows in feeling without reacting harshly. Leadership shows in sitting with another's frustration without mirroring it. Wisdom shows in staying present in discomfort long enough to learn from it. Someone who leads with emotional insight becomes more patient with others. They stop expecting perfection, because they have faced their own flaws and come out kinder. They do not confuse error with rebellion. They still correct, but without contempt. Without making people small.

They do not need to be adored. They want to be understood, and to understand in return. That posture changes the room. People relax. They stop pretending. They speak more plainly. They share what they would have held back, because they sense it is safe. Truth, messy or awkward, is not punished here. It is welcomed.

The emotionally intelligent leader listens beyond the words. They notice tension in a tone, weariness in someone's shoulders, guardedness in someone's eyes. They do not rush to diagnose, but they pay attention. They become stewards of the emotional current running beneath the surface, not to control it, but to care for it. Slowly, the culture shifts. People speak more honestly. They ask for help faster. They extend grace, because they have received it. Loyalty grows, not from pressure, but from shared humanity.

This kind of leader does not inspire from a distance. They meet people where they are. In that meeting, others find strength they did not know they had, not because it was demanded, but because it was safe to reveal. These leaders also leave room for reflection. They invite feedback, not because it is easy, but because they need it. They want to see themselves clearly, even when it stings. They do not wait for a breakdown to examine their ways; they do the work when the water is calm. And that habit becomes contagious. Others begin asking themselves, "How did I handle that? What can I learn here?" Not out of fear, but out of a quiet hunger to grow.

That is when the crew sharpens, but without cruelty. Ambition rises, but without self-serving edges. Collaboration deepens without silencing individuality. The work improves, not through pressure, but through alignment. Over time, morale lifts. Turnover slows. Meaning deepens, not from perks or posters, but from belonging; to each other, to the mission, to the moment. And it all begins because one person chose to lead not only with knowledge, but with care.

So let the leader begin not with control, but with self-awareness. Tend to your inner world, not perfectly, but honestly. Not to be impressive, but to avoid harm. Feel without being shaken. Speak without overpowering. Pause, and let others breathe too. Because the heart that governs itself with wisdom becomes a steady light in uncertain waters. And from that light, others find their way.

I OWN MY CHOICES. I SPEAK TRUTH ABOUT MY ACTIONS. IN DOING SO, I EARN THE TRUST THAT HOLDS THE CREW TOGETHER.

Accountability

No one can lead others well until they have learned to answer for themselves. Shifting blame forfeits trust. Hiding behind titles or excuses builds nothing that lasts. But the one who takes responsibility, quietly, fully, without delay, earns something rare: respect that cannot be bought, and authority that does not need to be performed. A leader's strength is not in always being right, but in always being accountable.

To lead is to bear weight, not just the results of your own choices, but the outcomes of those entrusted to your care. When something gets missed, when a promise slips, when a mistake surfaces, it is the leader who steps forward. Not to lecture. Not to vanish. But to say, "This begins with me." That is not weakness, it is weight carried the way it should be. And the crew notices.

They begin to move differently, not from fear, but from alignment. Because what is modeled with honesty tends to be mirrored. A team will pick up on what is allowed, what is praised, what is ignored. If the leader ducks accountability, others learn to hide. If the leader owns what is theirs, others start to do the same. The wise leader sets the tone early: clear expectations, consistent principles, space for questions. They do not assume others will "get it" without clarity. They name what matters. They listen when confusion rises. They adjust the plan when the path changes. They do not measure success by numbers alone, but by character under pressure.

Accountability, when lived with integrity, becomes more than correction; it becomes culture. A shared way of working. A common rhythm. In that kind of crew, mistakes are not buried. They surface early, while still easy to fix. Problems are not passed along in silence, they are faced. Responsibility does not always flow upward; sometimes it is handled right where it began. This is not about being flawless. It is about being mature.

The leader who builds this kind of culture holds themselves first. Quick to admit fault. Generous in giving credit. Firm in standards, but never above them. They ask the harder questions of themselves before asking them of anyone else. And where accountability lives, fear fades. People speak more freely. They step into decisions with more confidence. They ask, "How can I fix this?" instead of "Whose fault is it?" There is less hiding. More shared ownership. And from that, more progress.

But accountability cannot survive on criticism alone. It must be paired with recognition. The thoughtful leader points out what went right. Not to flatter, but to honor. Praise, when it is real and specific, strengthens more than correction ever could. Effort is seen. Wins are shared. Even the quiet work gets its moment. In that environment, excellence rises, not because it is demanded, but because it feels possible.

Over time, something deeper forms. Trust that does not need to be rebuilt every week. Trust that grows slowly, through a thousand small acts of follow-through. So let the leader be slow to point fingers, quick to carry their share, and faithful in finishing what they start. Let them keep their hand on the wheel, not only when things go right, but especially when they do not. Let them remain present when the winds change, when the sails tear, when the crew falters. Because that is when accountability truly shows itself.

Anyone can take credit when the sea is calm. But the leader who shows up when things break, who still takes responsibility when eyes are searching for someone to blame, that leader is remembered.

I THINK BEYOND THE MOMENT, KEEPING OUR EYES ON THE LONG HORIZON AND ENSURING OUR DAILY STEPS LEAD SOMEWHERE WORTHY.

Strategic Thinking

The wise leader does not see only what is near. They lift their eyes to the horizon. They are not consumed by the task at hand, but they do not forget it either. They hold both the detail and the destination. Their hands stay in the work, but their mind keeps reaching forward. They are not ruled by urgency. They move from something deeper: understanding. They choose not what is quickest, but what is lasting. That is the work of strategic thought — not to escape the moment, but to give it meaning.

Someone who leads with vision does not act without direction. Each word, each step, each choice fits within a larger frame. They notice patterns others miss. They wait when many rush. They prepare while others scramble. And in that preparation, clarity begins to surface. Strategic thinking does not depend on instinct alone, and it does not wait for perfect data. It listens, studies, learns. It draws as much from failure as from success. It looks not only at what is happening, but at where it is heading if nothing changes. It asks: Where are we going? What does this choice make possible, or close off, for those who come next?

But strategy is not rigidity. The course can shift without losing the mission. The direction can adjust without unraveling the intent. And the team, sensing that steadiness, begins to trust not just the plan, but the person behind it. Strategic thinking requires restraint — the ability to say "not yet" when shortcuts tempt, "not now" when distractions shout, and "not this" when a path drifts from values. And it requires courage: the courage to name risks, to face what might fail, to pursue what others do not yet see.

The leader who thinks in this way teaches their team to think this way too. They invite better questions and wider thinking. They give permission to pause before charging ahead, to wonder, Is this the right work? Or just the familiar work? They do not punish doubt. They sharpen it. They make space for it. They show that curiosity is not disruption, but care — proof someone wants to think deeply. Over time, the crew's perspective shifts. They begin to connect their piece to the larger whole. They move less like solo workers and more like a unified team, rowing in rhythm, eyes not only on the water, but on the distant shore.

Strategic leaders bring direction to effort. They align energy with aim. They do not scatter the crew's strength across every possible task. They choose the essential few over the frantic many. They ask not just what must be done, but why it matters. They know this: it is not intensity that moves a ship the fastest. It is alignment.

But strategy is not theory alone. It has to hold under pressure. Plans are tested by storms. Assumptions are exposed when the unexpected rolls in. That is where you learn whether the thinking was shallow or deep. The leader builds with layers. They do not try to control every wave, but they prepare for its arrival. They think ahead of the test so the test does not break the mission. They train the crew to adapt. They swap assumptions for contingencies. They make resilience part of the plan.

In this way, strategy becomes more than a document. It becomes culture. It shapes how the crew speaks, chooses, and measures. It spreads not through instruction, but through example. It becomes a compass passed quietly from one person to another. And as this culture takes root, something shifts. The crew stops waiting for instruction. They start seeing what needs to be done, and they do it, not because they were told, but because they believe in the direction. They begin to lead in their own ways, because now, they see.

So let the leader rise above distraction. Let them resist the rush that steals clarity. Let them guide not only with tasks, but with truth. In the end, it is not the ship's speed that decides if it reaches home. It is whether someone had the vision to steer it there. And the one who sees far gives meaning to every mile.

I MEET HARDSHIP NOT WITH NOISE, BUT WITH QUIET RESOLVE, ROOTED IN THE CONVICTION THAT SOME THINGS ARE WORTH STANDING FOR.

Courage

Courage makes no sound when it enters. It slips in through the quiet door, when no one is watching. Not the kind that brags or beats its chest, but the kind that stays put long after the crowd has gone. The real test of leadership is not how someone acts when all is well. Anyone can steer a ship in calm waters. But when the sky blackens, when the stars vanish, when nothing is clear and everything is loud, something else is required. Not charm or ease, but strength, quiet, often lonely strength. The kind that does not show itself in big speeches, but in a small, steady choice to do what is right, even when wrong would be easier.

There is bravery in big acts, sure. But courage lives just as often in the quiet no, the unpopular yes, the decision to hold your shape when everyone is pushing you to fold. To lead with courage is to enter rooms where your views will not be echoed, and speak anyway. It is to stay grounded when the ground beneath you shifts. Not rigid, but resolved. Not loud, but steady.

Courage is not recklessness, and it is not the absence of fear. It is what holds steady even when fear is present. The one who leads must learn when to step forward, when to wait, and when to simply stand, unwavering, even when no one claps. Each time that choice is made, the soul is shaped. Not all at once, but over time, that steadiness becomes a spine. And others lean on it.

Those under a leader's care do not find courage in slogans. They find it in example, in what a leader does when things go sideways. How blame is handled. How pressure is met. How truth is spoken, even when it stings. They feel it in the calm voice during chaos. In the leader who does not grab credit, but does not back away when the hard choice lands in their lap. And something shifts in them, too.

Sometimes courage is obvious, clear as day. Other times it is quiet: a leader shielding someone without saying a word, taking the hit to protect someone not in the room, or admitting flat out, without excuse, "I got it wrong." That kind of steadiness, lived and not just said, builds something solid. People begin to share ideas they once kept quiet. They speak up in tough rooms. Not because the risk disappears, but because it is safe to try, even to fail. Because failure is not final here. It is part of the work.

Leaders who create that kind of space do not stumble into it. They know the cost. They have stood in hard places and stayed. And when others see it, really see it, they begin to rise. They do not wait for permission. They find their own voice. They challenge with kindness. They lean into discomfort because they have seen it modeled.

A crew shaped by courage is not perfect. It is not polished. But it holds. It pulls each other through. It disagrees without dividing. It moves with purpose, not pressure. Leadership like this asks more than talent, more than charisma. It asks for presence, for consistency, for grit that shows up again and again when no one is watching, when no one is scoring points. And it asks for compassion too. That justice be wielded not like a sword, but like a compass. That care be given not as performance, but as priority. Because real courage is not cold. It feels deeply. It just does not flinch when things get hard.

Over time, courage becomes part of the air. Not something people name, but something they breathe. The leader is not idolized, but trusted. And when the storm hits, the crew does not scatter. They close ranks. They hold.

So let the one who leads not fear difficulty. Let them not shrink from the long road. Let them walk it upright, knowing the path they carve will be the path others follow. And when that moment comes, and it always does, when integrity is tested and no applause can be heard, let them stay. Hold the line. And in that stillness, others will find their own courage waking up. And they, too, will carry it forward.

I SPEAK PLAINLY, THAT THOSE WITH ME MAY SEE THE COURSE AHEAD AND UNDERSTAND WHY WE SAIL IT.

Communication

The voice of a true leader is not measured in volume or polished language. It is found in clarity, quiet and honest clarity that steadies more than it stirs. Great leaders are not speaking to impress. They are speaking to connect, to align, to bring light where confusion gathers. Most breakdowns do not happen because of the storm. They happen quietly, when people think they are aligned but are not. That is why a leader cannot just talk. They must check: is everyone seeing the same thing? They must become the clarifier, not only of tasks but of meaning, of values, of purpose. Not shouting from ahead, but inviting others to walk beside them.

At its best, communication is not about delivering facts. It is about revealing truth. It is not just about making sense, it is about making someone feel understood. That kind of clarity takes work. You do not stumble into it. It is built, word by word. Like choosing sails for a long journey, you do not just want them full of wind, you want them pointed the right way.

But no one communicates well without first learning how to listen. And not just hearing noise, but real listening; the kind that drops assumptions, slows judgment, and notices not only the words but the way they are said. The pause before the answer. The slight shift in tone. The thing left unsaid. A leader who listens like that creates space. And in that space, people stop performing and start speaking. That is where trust begins.

Clarity does not mean certainty. A confident voice can still be empty. But a clear message, grounded, steady, human, has weight. Even if it is hard to hear, it lands gently. And over time, it earns something louder voices rarely do: loyalty. The most powerful communication includes the why. Not just what needs doing, but why it matters. Without that, the work feels hollow. But when people understand the stars they are sailing toward, the grind becomes a calling. They do not just give their time, they give themselves.

Purpose needs plain language. Big words can blur things. They might sound impressive, but if people walk away unsure of what to do, the message missed the mark. People do not need polished poetry. They need clear direction. And when that direction is simple and true, it sticks.

Correction is where communication gets tested. Kindness is easy when everything is smooth. But when things go sideways, tone either builds trust or breaks it. A good leader does not correct to shame. They correct to lift. They separate the mistake from the person and speak to both with truth and with grace. And when praise is due, they give it without fuss but with intention. Not as flattery, but as fuel. "I saw that. It mattered." That kind of recognition can carry someone for months.

Not everything is said out loud. People notice pauses, body language, the way you walk into a room. If a leader says one thing but lives another, the message collapses. If they ask for honesty but bristle when it comes, the crew learns to stay quiet. So the leader's life must speak before their voice does. Their tone, their timing, and even their stillness all carry meaning. If there is warmth in the eyes and steadiness in the step, people lean in. If not, they pull back.

In a team shaped by this kind of leadership, communication becomes culture. People speak up without fear. They disagree without tearing down. They ask questions. They offer input. Not because they are told to, but because the space feels open enough to do so. Tools and technology can help share a message, but they cannot carry its soul. The wise leader chooses the channel that fits the moment. Sometimes a message can be written. Sometimes it has to be face to face. The point is not convenience. It is connection.

And that is the heart of it. Communication is not a skill you master and then move on from. It is a daily practice, a choice to be present, to mean what you say, to hold back when words are not needed and to step in when clarity is missing. Because when words are true and motives are clear, something solid takes root between speaker and listener. That is where trust begins.

Once trust lives between two people, leadership shifts. It stops being about authority. It becomes a shared journey. So let us speak plainly. Let us listen like it matters. Let us remember: what we say either builds or breaks. And if we build with care, if we communicate not to perform but to understand, even the hardest days become bearable. And the crew becomes not just a team, but a force that moves as one.

I GIVE THANKS OFTEN AND WITHOUT PROMPTING, KNOWING THAT RECOGNITION LIFTS THE SPIRIT AND STEADIES THE HAND.

Gratitude

The leader who grows wise does not rest only on yesterday's understanding, and they do not stand tall on their own achievements. They see each day as an open page, each moment as a gift. Gratitude shapes their view. They recognize lessons in success and failure, and they see the people around them not as cogs, but as companions worth honoring. They do not mistake title for wisdom, nor accomplishment for entitlement. Their eyes remain watchful, not for applause, but for instruction, and their heart remains thankful for what each moment gives.

Gratitude keeps a leader teachable. They do not claim to already know, because they value what others bring. They listen not just to experts but to beginners, grateful for fresh eyes that catch what experience overlooks. They honor the one who finds a better way. They thank the one who asks the hard question. They acknowledge the unseen work, the small effort that carries the team forward. Gratitude sharpens their attention and softens their pride.

The leader who practices thankfulness aloud builds something more than morale. They build trust. A simple "I saw that, thank you" can carry someone for weeks. Recognition becomes fuel, not flattery. And when correction is needed, it lands better in a culture where gratitude has already been spoken. People learn that their value is not erased by a mistake. They stay open, because they know their effort is seen.

This posture spreads. Gratitude is contagious. When the leader thanks, the crew starts thanking too. Meetings shift. Conversations loosen. People notice what is going right instead of only pointing at what is wrong. Gratitude creates space for honesty, because people feel valued before they speak. It makes collaboration easier, because appreciation clears the tension pride creates.

Over time, gratitude becomes more than manners. It becomes culture. It shapes how people see one another, how they handle conflict, how they push through difficulty. Work stops being just work; it feels like contribution. Effort stops being measured only by results; it is honored for intent and persistence.

A leader marked by gratitude does not see people as replaceable parts. They see them as fellow travelers. They thank in public, but also in private. They give credit freely. They point out what went well, not as a tactic, but as truth. And in doing so, they turn small moments into anchors, reminders that worth does not disappear when things get hard.

In the end, gratitude builds resilience. Crews shaped by it face storms with steadier hearts. They do not scatter at the first sign of trouble, because they know their work matters and their presence matters. They have heard it, often enough to believe it. Gratitude binds them together, lifting the ordinary into meaning.

So let the leader remember to thank. To notice. To honor. Not once in a while, but daily. Let gratitude be spoken plainly, lived honestly, carried quietly in both voice and action. Because when a leader leads with gratitude, the crew does not just follow. They belong. And from that belonging, strength grows.

I COMMIT TO LEARNING, NOT AS A TASK TO COMPLETE, BUT AS A WAY OF BEING, FOR MY GROWTH AND FOR THEIRS

Continuous Learning

The leader who would grow wise does not rest on yesterday's understanding. They see each day as an open page, each moment a chance to learn again. They do not mistake title for knowledge, nor age for wisdom. Their eyes stay watchful, not for applause, but for instruction in every success, every failure, every quiet exchange.

Learning is not a chapter to close or a prize to claim. It is a habit of attention, a way of walking through the world with ears open and eyes that still wonder. The leader who understands this devotes themselves to steady study, careful observation, honest reflection, and the slow gaining of insight. They read not for performance but for clarity. They listen not only to masters of the craft but to beginners too, because they know fresh eyes often see what the familiar miss. They watch for patterns, ask better questions, and allow answers to come in their own time.

The one who believes they already know has already stopped growing. They may still steer the ship, but only by habit, not by intent. Their hands are at the wheel, but the course quietly slips away. But the leader who remains teachable becomes like water, able to move, to bend, to flow around what once would have stopped them. Their mind stays quick, not from cleverness, but from openness. They are not rigid. They adjust their bearings when the winds shift, and they help the crew do the same.

And they do not keep this path to themselves. They honor the one who explores a wiser method. They walk with patience beside the slow learner. They hand down the charts they once needed, offering tools not as trophies but as gifts. They invite honesty, the freedom to say, "I have not figured this out yet." And when someone finally admits, "I am not sure," the leader does not rush to fix or judge. They guard that moment, make space for it. No eye rolls. No hurry. Just quiet permission to keep going. Real learning begins not with certainty, but with honesty. People only share that kind of truth when they know it will not be used against them.

The leader who admits they are still figuring it out shows more than humility. They show the crew what growth looks like. No need to announce it. Just the way they say, "I am still sorting this out," or, "Let me try again," sets the tone. And others pick it up. They do not need to demand growth; they model it. The crew watches how they listen, how they test, how they adjust when something fails. They learn to trust not in perfection, but in presence.

From that trust, something rare blooms. Ideas surface earlier. Challenges are spoken plainly. Honesty makes space for curiosity, the steady kind, not the scramble for shortcuts but the deeper wondering: "Is there a better way to do this?" Little by little, better ways appear. Not because someone made a big speech about innovation, but because the room got quiet enough for new ideas to breathe.

A culture of learning is not noisy. It does not boast of its brilliance. It listens more than it talks, and it reflects before reacting. Slowly, the crew enters a shared pursuit of better. When mistakes happen, as they always will, the learning crew leans in instead of away. They examine. They adjust. They grow. Errors become raw material for wisdom, not reasons to retreat.

The leader does not stand apart from this process. They are among the crew, learning too. Not for praise, but for principle. Because the health of the crew begins with the health of the one guiding it. When the leader admits the cost, the time, the uncertainty, the bruising of pride, their honesty invites courage in others. The crew begins to see that growth is not for the gifted, but for the willing.

There is a steadiness in this. A quiet strength. The leader who keeps learning becomes more than skilled. They become grounded, discerning, able to adjust without losing their way. And the crew, watching that rhythm of humility and resolve, steps into the same posture. They seek knowledge not to impress, but to contribute. They push boundaries not to grab credit, but to make things better for everyone. They begin to lead in small ways, not because they were told, but because they are ready.

This is the fruit of continual learning. Not just improvement, but transformation. Let the leader stay curious. Let them return again and again to the question, "What more can I understand?" Let them value the journey of becoming, not for what it adds to a résumé, but for what it shapes in the soul. And let that learning become the tide that lifts every voice aboard.

I rise again when I am knocked down, and in doing so, I show my crew how we carry on, not unscarred, but unbroken.

I RISE AGAIN WHEN I AM KNOCKED DOWN, AND IN DOING SO, I SHOW MY CREW HOW WE CARRY ON, NOT UNSCARRED, BUT UNBROKEN.

Resilience

Leadership is not proven when everything is going smoothly. It shows itself in the confusion, the detours, the unexpected breakdowns. When the map no longer matches the terrain, the leader stays steady, not because it is easy, but because someone has to.

Resilience is not bravado. Doubt is part of the path. What matters is the choice to move forward anyway, to keep going even when turning back would feel like relief. And when a leader falls, they rise — not because it did not hurt, but because they still believe the journey matters.

Leaders carry their own bruises. They know the disappointment of working hard and watching results lag. They keep showing up anyway. They do not let those moments speak the final word. They do not let hardship define them. Instead, they pay attention to what adversity might be trying to teach. Every setback holds something useful. Every failure is a mirror. The leader who listens to these moments, rather than dodging them, begins to build a strength that is quiet, steady, and real. It cannot be borrowed or faked. It is forged in long seasons, private effort, and recoveries no one sees.

A leader who has lived through enough storms becomes a kind of shelter. They become the calm voice when things unravel. They steady the crew without pretending to have all the answers. They never claim the road will be smooth, only that it is worth walking, and that no one will walk it alone. You do not really learn what kind of leader you are when things go as planned. That part is easy. The test comes when the map no longer fits the land, when everything shifts and nothing feels certain. That is when the crew looks to you, not for perfection, but for steadiness.

Resilience arrives quietly, without drumrolls or shouts. Most days it is just choosing to show up again, even with doubt whispering it would be easier to turn back. And sometimes you do fall hard. But you rise — not because the pain vanished, but because the work still matters.

There is no need to act tough all the time. Leaders feel the weight, the disappointments, the stretch of trying without seeing the result. Even then, they keep moving. Not to prove something, but because they believe the work still matters. Some strength only appears after sitting with discomfort and refusing to run. Not once, but over and over. In time, you stop needing to act unshaken. You grow roots.

When that shift happens — when you have lived through storms and still stand — you become more to those around you. Not just a guide, but a presence that helps hold them up. Not with speeches, but with steadiness. Mistakes stop being hidden. They are named, faced, and learned from. The crew stops bracing for blame. They begin showing up for each other, not because they must, but because trust has taken root.

Sometimes resilience looks like pausing long enough to catch your breath, admitting you are not sure what comes next, and walking forward anyway. But even this strength must be tended. The wise leader knows resilience is not built by pushing endlessly. It grows through rhythm — rest, reflection, laughter, learning. It grows by giving room to breathe, to shake off the day, to regain footing before the next step.

Leaders who notice what is not being said — the long silence, the tired voice, the posture that shows strain — create space for recovery. Not to coddle, but to care. Because a burned-out crew will not weather the storms ahead. But a supported crew, one that knows how to stumble and keep going, will always outlast urgency.

When progress finally comes, after all the starts and stalls, it feels different. It lasts. Because it came from people who endured, who adjusted, who kept trying when it would have been easier not to.

So let the leader be the one who shows up when the plan is still in pieces. The one who gets low to the ground and starts again, without rushing what takes time to mend. Let them meet the next challenge with steady eyes and an open heart, knowing each difficulty leaves behind something strong. Resilience is not about escaping struggle. It is about refusing to let it define you. And when a leader models that, rising not bitter but wiser, the crew does too.

Let them rise, and let that rising stir something forward in everyone watching.

I PRACTICE FAIRNESS, NOT BY FAVOR OR WHIM, BUT BY HOLDING ALL TO THE SAME LIGHT, EQUAL, SEEN, AND RESPECTED.

Fairness

A leader, if they would be just, must look upon each person with equal regard, not as parts to be used, but as people to be honored. Fairness is not a task to check off, nor a rule to enforce. It is a disposition, a way of seeing and acting that refuses to bend to bias or personal gain.

They do not favor the loudest voice, nor the one most like their own. They listen with balance. They weigh with care. And once they have judged a matter rightly, they hold to it, even when it costs them. Fairness is not only the absence of favoritism. It is the steady presence of principle.

To be fair is to walk the harder road. It means looking beyond friendship, past offense, and hidden assumptions. It means holding each person to the same standard and offering each the same dignity, whether praised or unknown, agreeable or difficult. The fair leader sets no traps. They make no backroom deals. They do not tilt the field for their own benefit, nor do they demand loyalty before giving justice. They speak plainly. They act openly. Their crew knows where they stand, and that steadiness becomes their strength.

They give space to quiet voices. They do not dismiss a concern because of who raised it. They do not let mood or preference tip the scale. When fairness is present, trust follows. Not all will agree, but most will understand. And in that understanding, a kind of peace forms, not of sameness, but of respect.

The fair leader also welcomes scrutiny. They are willing to revisit a decision if shown it was wrong. They do not cling to pride, but adjust out of honor. They know that equity is not always sameness. Some will need more time, more guidance, more support. They offer it not as charity, but because fairness demands it. Because fairness is less about giving everyone the same input, and more about ensuring each person has a real opportunity.

Their presence becomes a mirror. The crew, seeing fairness modeled, begins to practice it in turn. In disputes, in meetings, in choices both large and small, a spirit of even-handedness begins to grow. But fairness must be guarded, for it fades easily under pressure. It is easier to reward those we like, to overlook those who press us. The leader must watch themselves closely in moments of disappointment or conflict.

Let them ask: Would I treat another the same? Am I holding all to the same light? Am I acting from principle or preference? And if they find a shadow in their answer, let them correct it, not tomorrow, but today.

The conscience of the leader becomes the compass of the crew. If that conscience is clean, the path ahead, though never without trouble, will at least be straight. To lead with fairness is to lead without hidden hands or double standards. It is to create an environment where trust is not demanded but earned, where each person belongs not because of favors, but because they were treated justly.

So let the leader walk with even feet, speak with a clear voice, and judge with steady hands. Let them weigh truth over comfort, merit over mood. Favoritism will never hold a crew together. Fairness will. And in that fairness, the whole becomes stronger than any one part.

Charting Your Leadership Legacy

Leadership is not a title to be given or a finish line to cross. It is a way of walking, a way of seeing, and most of all, a way of being. One does not arrive at it. One becomes it.

With each tenet explored, we have not merely collected virtues, but uncovered truths that ask for daily return. Truths that will not sit quietly on the shelf, but call to be lived in word, in deed, and in moment.

Integrity taught us to hold fast, to choose what is right even when it costs, even when no one sees. Vision gave us direction, not just goals but the kind of far-sight that cuts through fog and doubt and says, "Still, we go." Courage showed up quiet, when fear was loud and the easy way was near. It reminded us that fear does not disqualify; it shows where courage is needed most.

Humility softened the edges. It brought us back to earth, showed us the strength in saying, "I was wrong," and the wisdom in asking, "What do you see that I do not?" Collaboration reminded us we were never meant to steer alone, that the great leader does not drown out voices but draws them in. Encouragement taught us to lift others, not for show, but because they matter.

Resilience met us when the wind changed and the plan unraveled, teaching us that setbacks are not shameful, but part of the voyage. Fairness steadied us when emotions tilted the scales, reminding us to lead with even hands and clear eyes. Emotional intelligence showed us how to read not only words, but tone, silence, and posture, giving us grace to stay when it would be easier to retreat.

Gratitude gave us breath. It slowed us enough to say, "Thank you," and mean it, reminding us that behind every success is a crew who gave something of themselves. Accountability asked us to own our part, in failure and in success, requiring of ourselves what we expect of others. Continuous learning reminded us we are always becoming, and that the most dangerous thought is to believe we already know enough.

These are not lessons to admire. They are paths to walk. And they must be walked again tomorrow.

So let us walk them — imperfectly, but earnestly. Quietly, but with resolve. Let us be the kind of leaders whose legacy is not recorded in reports or titles, but in the steadiness of our presence. In the lives made better because we chose to go first, and to go well.

Let the leader chart their course for responsibility, not recognition. Let them be known not for the spotlight they claimed, but for the light they kindled in others.

May you lead with a steady hand, a soft heart, and an unshakable core. And may your leadership not end with you, but ripple outward, carried on in those you guided, and in those they will one day guide.

This is your legacy. Carry it well.

Living the 20 Tenets of Great Leadership

I lead with integrity, choosing the honest course even when the easier path lies in reach.

I create space for truth to be spoken without fear, where voices are received with patience and heard without judgment.

I empower others through trust, giving responsibility not as a burden but as a path to excellence and strength.

I live the standard I set, letting my actions speak louder than any command or claim.

I cast a vision both steady and clear, a guiding light that gives purpose to each task and meaning to the voyage.

I embrace humility, acknowledging where I fall short and meeting each tide with a mind ready to grow.

I support and encourage my crew, celebrating their victories and walking beside them through the hard weather.

I foster unity, not through sameness, but by honoring difference, shaping a whole stronger than its parts.

I listen with care, hearing not only words but the heart behind them, and letting each voice be known.

I steer toward the greater good, choosing what serves the crew, even when the course is not the easiest to chart.

I remain flexible and watchful, adjusting our sails with foresight and grace as the winds shift.

I tend to my own spirit, understanding my emotions and extending empathy to those who journey with me.

I own my choices. I speak truth about my actions. In doing so, I earn the trust that holds the crew together.

I think beyond the moment, keeping our eyes on the long horizon and ensuring our daily steps lead somewhere worthy.

I meet hardship not with noise, but with quiet resolve, rooted in the conviction that some things are worth standing for.

I speak plainly, that those with me may see the course ahead and understand why we sail it.

I give thanks often and without prompting, knowing that recognition lifts the spirit and steadies the hand.

I commit to learning, not as a task to complete, but as a way of being, for my growth and for theirs.

I rise again when I am knocked down, and in doing so, I show my crew how we carry on, not unscarred, but unbroken.

I practice fairness, not by favor or whim, but by holding all to the same light, equal, seen, and respected.

Epilogue

You were not placed at the helm to command the waves, but to steady hands that tremble in their rise. Not to boast of the course, but to hold fast when it is lost and found again. You are not called to be praised, but to lift those who walk beside you. To pass quietly through the storm so others may find their strength in your calm.

True leadership does not leave applause behind, but the echo of courage awakened in another. It does not build monuments, but leaves the quiet proof that someone believed, and so another dared to follow. You are not the hero in their story. You are the one who reminded them they could begin. Who walked first, not for glory, but so no one would have to walk alone.

The journey is not finished. The sea still shifts. But because of you, there is one more light to steer by, one more soul who will not turn back. Go gently, and go bravely. Lead not for the sake of leading, but because the path is better walked together.

The voyage continues. And because of you, it continues with more hope, more purpose, and more light.

Captain S. Michael Hoelscher

www.ingramcontent.com/pod-product-compliance
Lightning Source LLC
Chambersburg PA
CBHW032059150426
43194CB00006B/578